Voices
Verses
Vices

Voices
Verses
Vices

Selected poems by

GRANT VAN WINGERDEN

This is an IndieMosh book

brought to you by MoshPit Publishing
an imprint of Mosher's Business Support Pty Ltd

PO Box 4363
Penrith NSW 2750

indiemosh.com.au

Copyright © Grant van Wingerden 2021

The moral right of the author has been asserted in accordance with the Copyright Amendment (Moral Rights) Act 2000.

All rights reserved. Except as permitted under the Australian Copyright Act 1968 (for example, fair dealing for the purposes of study, research, criticism or review) no part of this publication may be reproduced, stored in a retrieval system, or transmitted in any form or by any means, electronic, mechanical, photocopying, recording or otherwise, without the written permission of the publisher.

A catalogue record for this work is available from the National Library of Australia

https://www.nla.gov.au/collections

Title:	Voices Verses Vices
Author:	van Wingerden, Grant (1962–)
ISBNs:	978-1-922542-31-1 (paperback)
	978-1-922542-32-8 (ebook – epub)
	978-1-922542-33-5 (ebook – mobi)
Subjects:	POETRY / General; Australian & Oceanian

No individual in these poems is taken from real life. Any resemblance to any person or persons living or dead is accidental and unintentional. The author, their agents and publishers cannot be held responsible for any claim otherwise and take no responsibility for any such coincidence.

Cover concept by Grant van Wingerden
Cover design and layout by Ally Mosher at allymosher.com
Cover and internal images from Envato Elements and Adobe Stock

I dedicate this book (all the positive parts) to my children, Johan and Morgaine, and to my wonderful partner, Astrid Stephens, who has brought all this into shape.

Acknowledgements

I wish to thank Joy for reading to us as children and cultivating a keen interest in escaping into a good book.

Thanks also to my Dad for ensuring that I gained experience in all the robust outdoor activities; even ones I no longer do.

The two people most responsible for ensuring I wasn't a writer starving in a garret are Perth's Brian Jones and Wollongong's then Deborah Edwards who helped and encouraged me in an office career taking me up to a middle management role.

Thanks to my colleagues at Poetry Kit who can always be relied on for a fine exchange of critiques.

A shout out through the crowd to great gifted musicians like Tim, Steve, Andrew, Hugh, Stu, and Matt, who helped to corral wayward early musings while contributing brilliant original music.

Contents

Acknowledgements vii

Volume I Resurrection of Wholesome Folly 1

One 3

Breathing In, Breathing Out 4

Dreams in Black and White 5

Artistically Inclined 6

Shop with Soul 7

Ideal ism 8

Living out of Tins 9

What in America Makes the Music?! 10

Rubberstamping a Genius 11

If They Ever Make Me a Statue 12

It's Funny You Should Say That 14

Now I Get It 15

Questions Remain 16

Trampolining for God 16

In Your Mirror 17

With You in National Spirit 18

Incapable of Further Expression 20

The Social Conditioning of a Gerontologist ... 21

Meditating on the Median Strip 22

Posting a Further Guard to the Complex 24

Keeping mum 25

Volume II Misanthropist's Picnic 27

Arch 29

Extremist Barbecue 30

The Humourist Who Woke Up Dead On A
Sunday (Of All Days) 31

Dramatic Use of Irony 32

Anatomy of a Coup 33

Take a Seat, Mr Atheist 34

Barking Up the Wrong Tree 35

The Vanguard to Innocent Bravado 36

Suicides in the Pool 37

Lots of Luck 38

I've Been Past There 39

Bracket Creep 40

The Levitating Chiropractor 41

Opposite Extremes 42

Enough to Last a Lifetime 43

Volume I

Resurrection of

Wholesome Folly

One

I was standing in for genius
the last time that you saw me
I affected all kinds of things
when I endeared myself to you

And I was only one
The fabric fell about me

Your tears of shock
were for my beauty
Alas I cannot will
It to return

Oh I was one
My dreams were vivid

I was one

3 Voices Verses Vices

Breathing In, Breathing Out

It's the whisper in the wind it's the echo point shout
It's all the little things we can do without
It's the light of Truth without the shadow of a doubt
It's all the people of the world breathing in
and breathing out

Dreams in Black and White

Watch for the passions that start to excite
that determinant feeling 'pon approach of the night
Hold yourself close, it will be alright
when you go to sleep, you'll dream in black and white

That feeling will take you, you won't have to fight
You'll be free and floating as high as a kite
at perfect peace amidst perfect quiet
Keep your head down and head for the light
You'll be taken leave, you'll be in full flight
when you're asleep, all your dreams in black and white

You'll be there in seconds with second sight
your conscience is clear your friends locked up tight
you'll make it, you know that you're bright
your sleeping patterns, dreams in black and white

5 Voices Verses Vices

Artistically Inclined

Battling with a bottle of distilled intent
and a spreading pool of instilled dissent
The urge for withdrawal should be evident
as I write about destruction in your absence
I address my obsession in your dressing room
which is empty in the present tense
I am emptied of my common sense
My dreams are all of opulence
in the sense of being someone with someone
You are that someone, and am I the other one
then re-define refined and I will watch from behind
a stand-up mirror, see through curtains
and the blind
For the lonely and artistically inclined
For the lonely and artistically inclined

Shop with Soul

Have you ever wondered
about elevator muzak
shopping mall muzak
Nobody likes it
It's there to numb you

You're a suede demon Corinthian casual
and you shouldn't push trolleys
past plastic furniture
and recycled donuts

You should open a shop with soul
and invite us in for a look around
a cup of tea on the house
with a cat curled up at the counter
a dog dozing in the window
Then I'd like you more
I'd write postcards to friends in Goteborg
and tell them about you.

7 Voices Verses Vices

Ideal ism

I've been wishing for the ideal ism
I've gone fishing for the ideal ism
I've seen the schism
created by – isms
where people are imprisoned
by their – isms
Self-defeating like religion
But when you're looking through that prism
What's the fundamental ism
Will you seek the mystic ism
The social ism
Capital ism
Catholic ism
In the end it's whose decision
Marx missed the mark
yet Lenin carried on
in thirty four volumes
and still got it wrong
Illiterate peasants turned the lot to song
Made it big down in old Hong Kong
while searching for the ideal ism

8 Grant van Wingerden

Living out of Tins

Living in buried gravel with leather skin
This is where the yesterlife begins
We wouldn't change a single thing
Being from original sin
and living out of tins

Living in asbestos heat and grey dirt background
Living with chainsaw amusement, big tractor sounds
Living for the moment when the rain comes down
on this all our ground

Living out in tin sheds
Tales of overflowing tanks
12-bag crops and wholesale clearing
Where the bush life begins
Living out of tins
Where the hard life begins
Living out of tins

9 Voices Verses Vices

What in America Makes the Music?!

All are distant screams from violin corners
Blackface revivals in boroughs and ghettoes
Trodden-on troubadours awaiting the fate
Of a musical beginning and a silent finish
Grand tradition has taken them this far
And there they are
With history and homage in their heads
A bugle blaring out to unbelievers
A black and white beginning
and a colourful finish
Inseparable indiscreet America
What makes the music?!

Rubberstamping a Genius

We've used all the tools and we know
what they're for
We've seen the light, it comes through your door
We like the arrangements, we're booking in again
These keepsake mementoes will help us be friends
We've told all our old friends what our new
friends are like
Now they've cut off all contact. I think it's in spite
We draw our own pictures of the scenes that we see
and implanted in our brains is what it means
to be free
But honeymoon swashbuckling is too much for us
We spend our spare time rubber stamping a genius

If They Ever Make Me a Statue*

If I'm chosen to be chiselled
for the daring deeds I've done
Made ornamental and immortal
for the battles that I've won

I'll get no respect from the pigeons
or the tramps who camp at my base
Like all good inanimate objects
I'll finally know my place

If the very event of my passing
should see me etched in stone
The inspiration for an installation
that's made to stand alone

Gaze upon my granite visage
Marvel at my marbled thighs
Consider me cold and lifeless
Surveying from on high

12 Grant van Wingerden

Position me in the foyer
with monuments to other creeds
Unlikely as it is that my likeness
fulfils some kind of need

Admire my bronzed countenance
The thoughtful though conventional pose
Ponder the solemn authority
of one who appears to know

** First published in NSWNA staff magazine,
The Lamp, June 2002.*

It's Funny You Should Say That

I'm here sitting out a lonely summer
Warm white sand runs between my toes
I've left behind theological discussion
and you come up and say God knows

Now I Get It

Broken jigsaw in Dad's garage
Fright mask moulds and the fluorescent globe
Skate punk at precious thirteen
Mum switches channels
and picks up a strange voice
Like one you hear at the top of the stairs
in an old stage house
Nana and Pop read magazines
that are 20 years old - but they're free
and infested with morals
At least one member of the family
will want a microscope for Christmas
and will eat your biscuit when you're not looking

15 Voices Verses Vices

Questions Remain

The brilliant man has gone insane
his theories and notes blow down the lane
and wrap around a blind man's cane
who, being blind, can take no blame
for gathering them in and burning them

Trampolining for God

Oh to be exquisitely, honestly, physically
In love with moral fibre fabrication
Emptying our hearts and souls for a god
Who chooses to sit on woven blankets
Going native

In Your Mirror

In your mirror
I sit with my shoulders hunched
watching your paintings
In the past
I would have held you
and heard your promise
In the future
I will see you
in a different light
through a distant window
I will reflect
In your mirror

17 Voices Verses Vices

With You in National Spirit

I'm with you at the big rock
where a babe in arms spent time
I'm with you at the Top End
when they spin another line

I'm with you at the hangar
I'm with you at the dock
I'm with you all the way
in your corner of the world

I'll be signed up and sworn in
and pledge my allegiance
I will swear by your god
to stick to procedures

I'm polishing my rifle
Reading up my bible
Hunting down a mortgage
in a newly opened region

18 Grant van Wingerden

With you in national spirit
Fly those folks in with contented smiles
to be with you in national spirit

Government projects and foreign objects
Legal obligations to this country that you love

I'll be with you at the turnstiles
when they barricade the gates
I'll declare myself, my customs
and patiently I'll wait

All the way the USA, the CIA and TAA
I'll be lining up for more
Will you be there with me
when they begin to talk of war?

Well I'll be with you in national spirit
so fly those folks in with contented smiles
to be with us in national spirit

With you all the way in your
corner of the world
A flag upon your coffin
and another one unfurled

19 Voices Verses Vices

Incapable of Further Expression

He wears two hats
One's a stovepipe, one's a fedora
He drinks strawberry wine from a cracked decanter
He's read every tome in the public collection
He has an evil eye and a pet salamander
He dismissed Marx when he was thirteen
(Ralph Nader would come later)
He chops his own wood with a battle-ax replica
He chooses his food from surrounding wildlife
He ponders the death of the meaning of life
an hour before he retires
He thinks that God
is the ultimate fairy tale invention
He thinks that misogyny and race mythology
are two sides of a coin found in Asia Minor
And blesses his existence with rambling narratives
On folklore determinant
to lesser minions who worship the sun
And modern machinery
And catholic regeneracy
He wears two hats and he follows the sun

20 Grant van Wingerden

The Social Conditioning of a Gerontologist

The Legionnaires persist
in the ether and the mist
Ethereal terminology
Mystical abandonment
A frame for movement
Showing improvement
Old time religion beset with ill feeling
Neuralgia, nostalgia, a senile groping
Personal involvement and set method
Out of touch out of breath
An old heart atrophied from lone association
An old head considering but all is recollection
Waking up with a start feeling nervous
a few chosen words reworked for the service

Meditating on the Median Strip

I've lived all my life in a parked car
on the median strip of life
The supersonic jets fly overhead
carrying people to places they just have to go
And on the footpaths on either side
New fads rattle by day and night
They all end up at some stage
on the council tip
Till they're polished and placed back on the shelf
by an antique personality
with an antique mind
Analysts say that a motorcar is an extension
of a person's strength of character
I've never owned one
who wants to hide their feelings
on a major arterial highway
I let out all my aggression
on some bypass a long time ago
Spent all my insane cravings
on the businesses that opened and closed
On the edge of the freeway

22 Grant van Wingerden

People climb inside their cars
to forget themselves to find themselves
new directions
Wind up with a tattered map book
folded the wrong way
Stranded in some town with an untidy garage
Pieces go missing each time they set off
This is the best way
to watch life pass you by
Faster and faster all the time

23 Voices Verses Vices

Posting a Further Guard to the Complex

Trailing the suspect
Getting back to the subject
Fleshing out a prospect
Thinking up a concept
A share of the blame
Such a shame
Now it isn't much of a name
But it continues just the same
Turning a trick
Building in brick
Seven inches thick
Hear the locks click
Hear the clocks tick
A new guard is coming on duty

Keeping mum

I was only seven
playing next to the tank
Mum came out and
said she had something to tell me
She was leaving
My aunty would look after me

Even at that young age
I knew this couldn't be right
mothers don't leave their children

She was pushed out
but she didn't say that
It's the only part
I remember

how I was
uncomprehending

I didn't see her again
until I was eleven
when we snuck in a visit
and then seventeen

when I moved to the city

25 Voices Verses Vices

Volume II

Misanthropist's Picnic

Arch

Sex rites and stone walls
Have you lost your marbles
– or just your balls
Tracing fanatics
and shy little critics
The outline of architects
uncertain feelings
Michaelangelo's mirrored ceiling
Frustration enfolding
the shoulders Divine
The outlying figures
Temple dogs and temple gods
Tempered frustration
Resisted temptation
Prostrated redemption
In concentric circles
In uniform enclosure
Geometric solitude

Love me and leave me an offering

29 Voices Verses Vices

Extremist Barbecue

I shared my plate of sausages with someone
of different views
I said that I was satisfied; he said that just won't do
He'd gone and got religion, I went and got a chop
I asked how can you believe in God
When you can't find an honest cop
And how can you believe what you read is true
If there's another source that says it's not
He replied "We must have faith"
(when he returned from the loo)
For after all what else have we got
I demurred "Relying too much on faith is
everyone's mistake"
He grunted and poured too much sauce on the steak
As I helped myself to burnt baked potatoes
Intoning
"We must move on in our search for the truth"
He'd started talking to somebody else
And I got stuck into the booze

The Humourist Who Woke Up Dead On A Sunday (Of All Days)

His spirit has ascended to the badly painted ceiling
It squeezes through the crack
and comes out on the rafters
Boundless ideas for sketches here
Did you have one of those nights
you wake up dead in the morning?
It's always something you ate
or something you drank
or something you said
and shouldn't have
Priests on Sunday mornings
pray for the souls
that party late Saturday night

His spirit does its best impression
Almost brings the house down
Before fading into the frames
of those old flames
who are laughing last, at last

Dramatic Use of Irony

Ah so good to see you after so long away
You're a celebrated figure, I understand, today
Your succinct phrases have filled
their heads with praises
And the company you keep now is ever so deep
Would have the solution if they held the power
Growing older and more cynical at each passing hour
You love the detachment, their affectations
A constant source of inspiration
But I heard you once whisper "God pity me"
The writer who employs dramatic irony

Anatomy of a Coup

I'm collecting bottle tops on the
seashores of Paradise
There are notes written in the sand
that never wash away
Where up in the palace the fool is drowning
in his own bathtub

33 Voices Verses Vices

Take a Seat, Mr Atheist

I'm glad you're sure of nothing
There's nothing short of nothing
The carnival's closed forever
I've gathered my thoughts and left you alone
The walls are showing their age
Comments to go with a fast food mind

Take a seat, Mr Atheist
There's a new cult for you to shop
A place in the halls of the unpredictable
behavioural patterns changing
I love the way they make love
seem like a very good business
I love the twists and turns
that come when God is witness
I want to hold what cannot be
Smoke the bones of radical theology
Mr Atheist

Barking Up the Wrong Tree

Arf arf arf a loaf is better than none
Arf arf arf your luck son
Arf arf arf ah forget it
Arf the time's not worth the effort
Ah fer folks' sake
Arf arf arf arf
Ah fucken hell

The Vanguard to Innocent Bravado

We had a modern technology failure
And all the clocks in the ancient valley stopped
The eldest most trusted aldermen went in search
of sympathy
And wound up trapped in the tradesman's entrance
With fish'n'chips wrapped in unfulfilled contracts
And a group of babies that were left on doorsteps
Grew up to be military commanders
Shouting in time about civilian obligation
And somebody wanted a boardroom shuffle
With champagne and orange
And free pens and paper
To draw up a list of alternative demands
While the wild animals who escaped
the city ordinance
Floated and flapped and called and
One deaf mute
blindfolded for the occasion
Reenacted a seventeenth century curse
And the clocks were fixed

And all returned to normal

36 Grant van Wingerden

Suicides in the Pool

Fat white bodies heading for the blue strip
Taking in heavy chloride
A fine fine fine final sense of achievement
In backyard Las Vegas

Savage dogs and Persian cats prowl
On the artificial green banks
The undertaker's taking
Lifesaver training

And the pool is draining

II/ Fat cigars, fat bulging pockets
Word gets around
And ghouls gather upon the concrete

III/ They say the pool is haunted
Or that a whirlpool took them down
They say endless things about the rich
And the dead rich

Ha I even forget which banks they owned
But I know why they drowned

37 Voices Verses Vices

Lots of Luck

I channel tunnel vision to visit foreign shores
I start to go to pieces and end up in the wars
with the boring pragmatists busy making laws
There's safety in numbers, numbness in this safety
This philosophy of philistines filling up the texts
I will ramrod their Pseudo-Reason,
flick back the catch
Burn down High Society – y'gotta match

I've Been Past There

Lot #59's wife still turning her head
Sodom she says they refuse to be led
Deifying their own junk values
Drawing higher salaries
But all her many indiscretions
Wind up in True Confessions
And Patient Griselda she well knows the score
After all she lives next door
She's seen the way that they keep house
She keeps her own counsel; she's so devout
Lot #59's wife, a pillar of salt
Kept in the cellar over who was at fault

Bracket Creep

You've got cellular hearing
(and you've reached your ceiling)
You've got garden design
(you've got mouldy old clippings)
You have a right to your opinion
(to be published on demand)
You have the group to do it in
(and bring it back tomorrow)
You have the keepsake attitude
(you have the regal leanings)
You have it up to here
(and here and here and here)

Your well is deep, your cellar is deep,
your carpet is deep
But you're not deep
Bracket creep

The Levitating Chiropractor

The world is impatient, it quivers and it blows
Mistaken by the Millerites as in its death throes
I rest my case by the E-meter clicking
Now Ron is dead, Herbert is dead,
the thing keeps ticking
The Pontiff shakes his head and kisses brows
In halted English whispers "Who's sorry now?"

I could've been there
I could've shaken hands with strangers
With my poison arm still dangling
Laughed in your faces and spit in your eyes
Wound up the rack saying "Try this for size"
I could've shown you
What madness lies in souls of the unrested
Shining through those fearful crazy eyes
Right up to your wretched withered necks
Playing with your feelings about sex
I couldn't and I didn't
Say you're sorry
The levitating chiropractor takes a bow.

Opposite Extremes

Waking thoughts that came to nought and broken dreams
Walking home and driving out
Rife with self-confidence, riddled with doubt
Got religion made scientific proof
Found myself underground as high as the roof
Had to bottle in emotions, had to let off steam
Had to join the club to be by myself
Speaking in whispers in a dull roaring shout
Remain standing still always getting about
Feeling guilty knowing your right
Hiding in the darkness searching for the light
Channelling energies slumping in a chair
Searching for a maybe you know isn't there
Breaking apart with opposite extremes

Enough to Last a Lifetime

What's wrong with what I am
Do I not conform
to the city streets and squalor
to the published paranoia
Don't I blend in
with the breakdance remarks
Meaningless High Gloss
Should I be shouting
at a level with the traffic
Searching out sidelines
in the rubbish bins and side streets
in the parks with wicked bottles
Or should I go home
and leave you to this madness
It's hard taking camera shots
of decadence and poverty

Enough to last a lifetime

www.ingramcontent.com/pod-product-compliance
Lightning Source LLC
LaVergne TN
LVHW040202080526
838202LV00042B/3279